# Jack Ma:

# 199 Best Quotes from the Great Entrepreneur – Alibaba, E-Commerce, Future, Money, Failure and Success

*(Powerful Lessons from the Extraordinary People Book 3)*

edited by
Olivia Longray

ISBN: 9798551343462

Copyright © 2020. All rights reserved.

*"Never give up. Today is hard, tomorrow will be worse, but the day after tomorrow will be sunshine."*

— **Jack Ma**

# Contents

Introduction ..................................................................................... 5
Part 1: LIFE LESSONS ................................................................... 8
    Childhood & Upbringing ............................................................ 8
    Education ................................................................................... 10
    Difficulties Finding Jobs ........................................................... 12
    First Steps to Start a Business .................................................. 14
    Money & Revenues ................................................................... 17
    Happiness .................................................................................. 20
    The IQ of Love .......................................................................... 22
    Wisdom vs. Muscles ................................................................. 23
    The Cost of Deceit .................................................................... 24
    Being Jack Ma ........................................................................... 26
Part 2: INCREDIBLE PROJECTS ................................................. 29
    Alibaba Group ........................................................................... 29
    Dreams that Change the World ................................................ 33
    Investing in China ..................................................................... 34
    Supporting Young People ......................................................... 37
    The Impact of Technology ........................................................ 38
    Inspiring Philanthropy .............................................................. 40
    Artificial Intelligence ................................................................ 42
    The Internet & E-commerce .................................................... 44
    How to Change the Future ....................................................... 46
Part 3: SUCCESS LESSONS ......................................................... 49
    Put Customers First .................................................................. 49
    Choose to be Optimistic ............................................................ 51
    Never Give Up ........................................................................... 52
    Hire Smart People .................................................................... 54

- Learn from Other People's Mistakes ..................................................56
- Leaders Never Complain ...................................................................57
- Focus on Making Values .....................................................................59
- Don't Worry ..........................................................................................60

**Part 4: BRILLIANT ADVICE FOR ENTREPRENEURS ..........61**
- How to Build a Successful Company ................................................61
- Failure & Patience ................................................................................63
- Opportunities for Business Growth ..................................................64
- Women in Business ..............................................................................65
- Productivity Tips for Entrepreneurs .................................................66

**7 Book Recommendations from Jack Ma ...............................68**

**FREE book .........................................................................................69**

**Your Reviews ....................................................................................70**

**A Note on Sources ...........................................................................71**

# Introduction

Chinese billionaire Jack Ma, the founder of the internet giant Alibaba, is a man with an unusual biography. In an interview, he said that it is impossible to succeed in China if you do not have connections, political capital, or wealth. He didn't have any of those things when he started out.

How did he manage to become the man he is today? He is considered a superman, the Steve Jobs of China, and the godfather of Chinese entrepreneurship. Jack Ma's fortune is estimated at more than $50 billion and he is one of the top 20 richest people in the world.

Jack Ma (originally Ma Yun) was born in the city of Hangzhou to a very poor family and did not receive a remarkable education. In general, school was difficult for him, especially mathematics. Even now, the businessman has problems with the numbers and, if you give him financial statements, he will not understand much.

However, as a young student, he was interested in English. From the age of 12, he got up early every morning and, regardless of the weather, rode a bicycle to a hotel, where he worked as a free tour guide for foreigners, as a way to practice his English.

He did this for 8 years and he has stated that this time changed him profoundly. That was when Ma Yun became Jack. It was difficult for tourists to pronounce their guide's Chinese name, so they called him Jack, which was much more familiar to their Western ears.

After finishing school, he failed his university entrance exams twice and was only accepted to Hangzhou Teacher's University, which was considered the worst in the city. After graduating, he started looking for a job. But Jack Ma continued to have a hard time. He was turned down for jobs more than 30 times. The only place where he was able to get a job was his alma mater. Jack became an English teacher. He turned out to be a natural teacher and he loved the job, even though he only earned $12 a month.

Jack Ma saw his first computer at the age of 31 when he traveled to the United States as a translator with a trade delegation. There he learned about the Internet and the first word that Ma entered into a search engine was "beer". The search results included American beer and German beer, but no Chinese beer. When Jack Ma realized that there was no information about China on the Internet at all, he wanted to bring the Internet to his homeland.

First, he launched a website development company, and then, in 1999, he founded Alibaba in his apartment along with 18 partners. According to the businessman himself, before 2010, he had not personally written a single line of code or made a single direct sale to a customer. He bought his first computer at the age of 33.

This is how Alibaba's story began. Jack Ma calls his company "1001 mistakes". After overcoming many difficulties, he achieved success and became a blessing to the Chinese people. Now, Alibaba employs more than 65 thousand people.

Jack Ma envisioned a company that would live for at least 102 years. This initial vision implied that leadership at Alibaba would need to change more than once. And that is what happened. In 2019, Jack Ma retired as executive chairman of the Board of Directors and passed the role on to his successor. When asked about his plans for the future, the billionaire has said that he still considers himself young and will devote all his free time to teaching and philanthropy.

Jack Ma tries to be private about his personal life. He met his wife, Zhang Ying, in the late 1980s when he was studying at university. They have three children together. "Ma Yun is not a handsome man, but I fell for him because he can do a lot of things handsome men cannot do," said his wife.

# Part 1: LIFE LESSONS

## Childhood & Upbringing

1. "I don't have a rich or powerful father, not even a powerful uncle."

—*Jack Ma's speech at Peking University, 2014*

2. "As a young boy – even today – I never thought I would be here. When I look back, every problem I met when I was a kid benefited me."

—*CNBC, January 30, 2018*

3. "When I was 12 years old, I got interested in learning English. I rode my bike for 40 minutes every morning, rain or snow, for eight years to a hotel near the city of Hangzhou, about 100 miles southwest of Shanghai.

China was opening up, and a lot of foreign tourists went there. I showed them around as a free guide and practiced my English. Those eight years deeply changed me. I started to become more globalized than most Chinese. What I learned from my teachers and books was different from what the foreign visitors told us."

—*Inc., January 1, 2008*

4. "Nobody said that I would be a very capable person that would do something significant or meaningful in the future."

—*Forbes, May 7, 2014*

5. "The other event that fundamentally changed me was in 1979 when I met a family with two kids from Australia. We met and spent three days together and played Frisbee. We became pen pals. In 1985 they invited me to go to Australia for a summer vacation. I went in July, and those 31 days changed my life.

Before I left China, I was educated that China was the ... happiest country in the world. So when I arrived in Australia, I thought, 'Oh, my God, everything is different from what I was told.'"

—*Inc., January 1, 2008*

6. "Everything I'd learned in China was that China was the richest country in the world."

—*The New York Times, January 5, 2007*

7. "When I arrived in Australia, I realized it's totally different. I started to think you have to use your own mind to judge, to think."

—*The New York Times, January 5, 2007*

## Education

8. "How can we teach kids to be more creative and do things that machines cannot do? Machines have chips, but human beings have hearts.... Education should move in this direction."

*—Jack Ma at the World Economic Forum in Davos, January 23, 2019*

9. "When you are 20 to 30 years old, you don't know what you're doing. You have a lot of ideas. You think you can do anything. But actually you can't."

*—The Financial Times, February 3, 2019*

10. "I failed at key primary school tests two times, and I failed three times for the middle schools. I applied for Harvard – 10 times rejected, and I told myself that someday I should go teach there."

*—Jack Ma at the Viva Tech conference in Paris, May 16, 2019*

11. "I flunked my exam for university two times before I was accepted by what was considered my city's worst university, Hangzhou Teacher's University. I was studying to be a high school English teacher. In my university, I was elected student chairman and later became chairman of the city's Students Federation."

*—Inc., January 1, 2008*

12. "A teacher should learn all the time; a teacher should share all the time. Education is a big challenge now – if we do not change the way we teach, thirty years later we will be in trouble.

We cannot teach our kids to compete with the machines who are smarter – we have to teach our kids something unique. In this way, 30 years later, kids will have a chance."

—Jack Ma at the World Economic Forum in Davos, January 24, 2018

13. "I am not good at math, have never studied management, and still cannot read accounting report."

—Deutsche Welle, September 10, 2014

14. "I have never written one code, never made one sale to a customer."

—Bloomberg, November 9, 2014

## Difficulties Finding Jobs

15. "Your first job is your most important. That doesn't mean it has to be your dream job or even one you particularly enjoy. But it does have to be one where you can learn from others and stretch yourself....

You should find a good boss that can teach you how to be a human being, how to do things properly, and stay there. Give yourself a promise: I will stay there for three years."

*—Jack Ma at the World Economic Forum in Davos, January 23, 2019*

16. "When I graduated, I was the only one of 500 students assigned to teach at a university. My pay was 100 to 120 renminbi, which is like $12 to $15 per month.

I always had a dream that when I finished my five years, I would join a business – a hotel or whatever. I just wanted to do something. In 1992, the business environment started improving. I applied for a lot of jobs, but nobody wanted me!"

*—Inc., January 1, 2008*

17. "I failed a lot. I applied to 30 different jobs and got rejected. I went for a job with the police; they said, 'You're no good.' I even went to KFC when it came to my city. Twenty-four people went for the job. Twenty-three were accepted. I was the only guy [who wasn't]."

—*Bloomberg Businesweek, January 30, 2015*

18. "I survived the corporate world for 20 years because I was a teacher in my former life."

—*Jack Ma at the World Economic Forum in Davos, January 23, 2019*

## First Steps to Start a Business

19. "In 1995, I went to Seattle as an interpreter for a trade delegation. A friend showed me the Internet there for the first time. We searched the word 'beer' on Yahoo and discovered that there was no data about China. We decided to launch a website and registered the name China Pages."

—*Inc., January 1, 2008*

20. "The first time I used the Internet, I touched on the keyboard and I found 'Well, this is something I believe, it is something that is going to change the world and change China.'"

—*Talk Asia, CNN, April 25, 2006*

21. "I borrowed $2,000 from my relatives, my brother-in-law and my parents to set up the company. I knew nothing about personal computers or e-mails.... That's why I call myself a 'blind man riding on the back of a blind tiger.'"

—*Inc., January 1, 2008*

22. "The day we got connected to the web, I invited friends and TV people over to my house. We waited for three and a half hours and got half a page. We drank, watched TV and played cards, waiting. But I was so proud. I proved the Internet existed."

—*CNN Business, September 9, 2018*

23. "We competed with China Telecom for about a year. The general manager of China Telecom offered to invest $185, 000 to do a joint venture. It was the most money I had ever seen in my life.

But unfortunately, China Telecom got five board seats. I got two board seats. Everything we suggested, they turned us down. It was like an elephant and an ant. I resigned. Then, I got an offer to come to Beijing and run a new government group to promote e-commerce."

*—Inc., January 1, 2008*

24. "My dream was to set up my own e-commerce company. In 1999, I gathered 18 people in my apartment and spoke to them for two hours about my vision. Everyone put their money on the table, and that got us $60,000 to start Alibaba.

I wanted to have a global company, so I chose a global name. Alibaba is easy to spell, and people everywhere associate that with 'Open, Sesame,' the command that Ali Baba used to open doors to hidden treasures in 'One Thousand and One Nights.'"

*—Inc., January 1, 2008*

25. "If Jack Ma and his team can be successful, so can 80% of the people in the world. Because we had almost nothing, but we believed in the future."

*—Jack Ma at the Viva Tech conference in Paris, May 16, 2019*

26. "There were three reasons why we survived. We had no money, we had no technology, and we had no plan. Every dollar, we used very carefully.... We expanded when we raised money from Goldman Sachs in 1999 and then Softbank Corporation in 2000."

*—Inc., January 1, 2008*

27. "I remember, in 2001, we went to raise some $3 million in venture capital in the U.S. and got rejected. So we've come back and raised a little bit more: $25 billion.

This is not money; this is the trust of the world, the trust of the people. They want us to do a better job and help more people. And they want to have a good return. So it puts more pressure on me."

*—Bloomberg Businesweek, January 30, 2015*

## Money & Revenues

28. "If you are still poor at 35, you deserve it."

—*Republic World, September 10, 2019*

29. "When we have money, we start making mistakes."

—*YourStory.com, November 17, 2019*

30. "People say I am one of the richest people in China, but I don't think it is my money. It is money that people have entrusted to you, and you want to spend it in a better, smarter way."

—*Forbes, December 2, 2019*

31. "When I graduated, I earned $20 a month, which was fantastic."

—*Time, September 23, 2014*

32. "Today, making money is very simple. But making sustainable money while being responsible to the society and improving the world is very difficult."

—*YourStory.com, November 17, 2019*

33. "You don't make mistakes when you don't have money.... When you have too much money, you will make a lot of mistakes."

—*Jack Ma at the University of Tokyo, December 6, 2019*

34. "I don't care about revenues."

*—YourStory.com, November 17, 2019*

35. "My favorite movie is 'Forrest Gump.' He said nobody makes money catching whales, people make money catching shrimps. Every time when I'm frustrated, I watch the movie."

*—Business Insider, June 20, 2019*

36. "I own no branded goods. I have no interest in cars. What interests me is whether I can create change in this world. [Bill] Gates donated $58 billion, and that is his contribution to society.... I feel that Gates is a very great man – by doing things such as these, he left an impact on the world."

*—Vulcan Post, May 22, 2015*

37. "When you have one million dollars, you're a lucky person. When you have 10 million dollars, you've got trouble, a lot of headaches. When you have more than one billion dollars or a hundred million dollars, that's a responsibility you have. It's the trust of people on you because people believe you can spend money better than the others."

*—Time, September 23, 2014*

38. "A lot of entrepreneurs don't make it in the end, not because they don't have money, but because they have too much money. When you try to solve problems with money, that is when your real problems start."

*—Jack Ma's speech at Stanford University, June 19, 2013*

39. "People are afraid to look me in the eye; everyone wonders how Alibaba became so powerful, how Jack Ma is so clever. After achieving some modest results, we run the risk of forgetting who we are because we're young, we're ordinary people."

*—Vulcan Post, May 22, 2015*

## Happiness

40. "I try to make myself happy because I know that if I'm not happy, my colleagues are not happy, and my shareholders are not happy, and my customers are not happy."

—*YourStory.com, November 17, 2019*

41. "Life is so short, so beautiful. Don't be so serious about work."

—*Entrepreneur, October 31, 2018*

42. "It doesn't matter how wealthy or powerful you are. If you can't enjoy the sunshine, you can't be truly happy."

—*YourStory.com, November 17, 2019*

43. "I don't want to die in my office. I want to die on the beaches."

—*Business Insider, June 20, 2019*

44. "I always tell myself that we are born here not to work, but to enjoy life. We are here to make things better for one another."

—*Jack Ma's speech at De La Salle University, October 25, 2017*

45. "Every day is uncertain. The only certain day was yesterday."

*—Medium, May 17, 2018*

46. "Life is like a box of chocolates. You never know what you're going to get."

*—Time, September 23, 2014*

47. "In China, the government doesn't trust the people, and the people don't trust the government. The media don't trust the people, and the people don't trust the media. Nobody is happy. The poor are not happy, neither are the rich. Why? Because we are living in a time of constant change."

*—Jack Ma's speech at Stanford University, June 19, 2013*

48. "These three, five years, it's definitely not me for whom I'm working. The happiest times of my life were when I only earned $92, during that time my beliefs were very simple: work for a few months more, earn a bit of money, then I can buy myself a bicycle.

In business today, one must have a spirit of openness, a mentality of sharing, a globalized outlook, and a sense of responsibility."

*—Vulcan Post, May 22, 2015*

## The IQ of Love

49. "To gain success, a person will need a high EQ. If you don't want to lose quickly, you will need a high IQ. And if you want to be respected, you need a high LQ – the IQ of love."

*—Jack Ma's interview for World Economic Forum, January 24, 2018*

50. "Don't be evil is not enough. We should do good things for the world. Do good things for the future."

*—Time, January 23, 2019*

## Wisdom vs. Muscles

51. "This century is about wisdom, not muscles."

—*Medium, May 17, 2018*

52. "I love Forrest Gump. People think he is dumb, but he knows what he is doing."

—*Business Insider, April 14, 2016*

53. "A peace talk is always difficult, always complicated."

—*Jack Ma at the D: All Things Digital conference in California, June 1, 2011*

54. "Only fools use their mouth to speak. A smart man uses his brain, and a wise man uses his heart."

—*Medium, September 12, 2019*

## The Cost of Deceit

55. "Never deceive others, in business or life. In 1995, I was deceived by four companies – four companies that are now closed. A company cannot go far by deceit."

—Business Insider, July 1, 2016

56. "It's an easy thing to hoodwink others – I can be a hypocrite and tell others, 'You're very hardworking, very diligent, persist for a few years and you'll definitely succeed.'

But in reality, the road you've just recommended is a dead end. I believe what this generation requires is for people to tell them the truth, for people to be honest with them at critical moments."

—Vulcan Post, May 22, 2015

57. "When I was a judge on 'Win in China' (a Chinese reality TV show where entrepreneurs compete for investments), there were several contestants who were very cute, their speeches were humorous and entertaining.... The people behind the show wanted to let them stay, saying that it would boost ratings.

[But] I said I ought to speak the truth because I believe that this show will leave a huge impact on a lot of budding entrepreneurs – both current and those five to ten years down the road. If I flatter them in my position and say what isn't truthful merely for the sake of entertainment, it would harm a generation of entrepreneurs."

—*Vulcan Post, May 22, 2015*

58. "Every fake product we sell, we are losing five customers. We are the victims of that. We never stop fighting.

The problem is the fake products today are of better quality and better price than the real names. They are exactly the same factories, exactly the same raw materials, but they do not use the names."

—*The Wall Street Journal, June 15, 2016*

## Being Jack Ma

59. "I am a very simple guy. I am not smart. Everyone thinks that Jack Ma is a very smart guy. I might have a smart face, but I've got very stupid brains."

*—Business Insider, July 1, 2016*

60. "I don't want to be liked. I want to be respected."

*—Sarasota Herald-Tribune, June 2, 2011*

61. "I'm just a purist. What is important in my life is that I can do something that can influence many people and influence China's development. When I am myself, I am relaxed and happy and have a good result."

*—Inc., January 1, 2008*

62. "Before I'm 50 years old, my job is making money. After I'm 50 years old, my job is spending money, helping others, because you can't spend all that money."

*—Business Insider, June 20, 2019*

63. "I'm a normal guy. I feel ashamed because I feel I'm stealing the contribution of my team. They made it; my job is more, 'Let's go do it.'"

*—The New York Times, January 5, 2007*

64. "What keeps Jack Ma awake at night? Nothing! If I don't sleep well, the problem will still be there. If I sleep, I have a better chance to fight it."

—*Jack Ma at the World Economic Forum in Davos, January 23, 2019*

65. "Alibaba is but one of my dreams. I'm still young."

—*The New York Times, September 10, 2019*

66. "I want to create one million jobs, change China's social and economic environment, and make it the largest Internet market in the world."

—*Inc., January 1, 2008*

67. "I will start a new chapter in my life. As a person that loves liveliness as much as me, I would not want to retire and leave the playground at such a young age. I just want to switch to another universe to have fun."

—*Forbes, September 11, 2019*

68. "I want to go back to teaching. Not to teach in one classroom, but to change the way we teach and what we teach. I want to make young people ready for the future."

—*Jack Ma at the Viva Tech conference in Paris, May 16, 2019*

69. "There's a lot of things I can learn from Bill Gates. I can never be as rich, but one thing I can do better is to retire earlier. I think some day, and soon, I'll go back to teaching. This is something I can do much better than being CEO of Alibaba."

*—Bloomberg, September 7, 2018*

70. "I'm not a fan of going to Mars. We need heroes like you [Elon Mask], [who want to go to Mars], but we need heroes like us [who will fix Earth]."

*—Jack Ma at the World AI Conference in Shanghai, August 29, 2019*

71. "I had always wished that I was born in a period of war. I could have been a general. I thought about what I could have achieved in war."

*—Forbes, May 7, 2014*

# Part 2: INCREDIBLE PROJECTS

## Alibaba Group

72. "Alibaba is not just a job. It's a dream. It's a cause. Let the Wall Street investors curse us if they want."

*—Business Insider, July 1, 2016*

73. "I was scared and had doubts [when I started Alibaba]. But I believed someone, if not us, would win. There are no experts of tomorrow, only of yesterday."

*—Jack Ma at the World Economic Forum in Davos, January 23, 2019*

74. "I call Alibaba '1,001 mistakes.' We expanded too fast, and then in the dot-com bubble, we had to have layoffs. By 2002, we had only enough cash to survive for 18 months. We had a lot of free members using our site, and we didn't know how we'd make money.

So, we developed a product for China exporters to meet U.S. buyers online. This model saved us. By the end of 2002, we made $1 in profits. Each year we improved. Today, Alibaba is very profitable."

*—Inc., January 1, 2008*

75. "The lessons I learned from the dark days at Alibaba are that you've got to make your team have value, innovation, and vision. Also, if you don't give up, you still have a chance. And, when you are small, you have to be very focused and rely on your brain, not your strength."

*—Jack Ma at the Clinton Global Initiative meeting in New York City, September 23, 2014*

76. "We got successful today not because we did a great job today – we had a dream 15 years ago."

*—Time, September 23, 2014*

77. "Google, Facebook, Amazon and AliBaba – are the luckiest companies of this century. But we have the responsibility to have a good heart and do something good. Make sure that everything you do is for the future."

*—Jack Ma at the World Economic Forum in Davos, January 24, 2018*

78. "We're in China today because I believe in one thing: global vision, local win. We designed the business model ourselves. Our focus is on helping small and medium-size companies make money.

We never copied a model from the U.S., like a lot of Chinese Internet entrepreneurs, did. We focused on product quality. It has to be 'click and get it.' If I can't get it, then it's rubbish."

*—Inc., January 1, 2008*

79. "Amazon is more like an empire – everything they control themselves, buy and sell. Our philosophy is that we want to be an ecosystem. Our philosophy is to empower others to sell, empower others to service, making sure the other people are more powerful than us.

With our technology, our innovation, our partners – 10 million small business sellers – they can compete with Microsoft and IBM."

*—CNBC, January 18, 2017*

80. "Our philosophy is using Internet technology we can make every company become Amazon."

*—CNBC, January 18, 2017*

81. "If we go to work at 8 a.m and go home at 5 p.m, this is not a high-tech company, and Alibaba will never be successful. If we have that kind of 8-to-5 spirit, then we should just go and do something else."

*—The Economic Times, September 25, 2014*

82. "Alibaba's vision, which will be driven by my successor CEO Daniel Zhang, is that by 2036 Alibaba wants to have a digital economy to create 100 million jobs, serve 2 billion consumers and support 10 million profitable businesses on our platform

We are working to enable global buy, global sell, global pay, global delivery and global travel for everyone."

*—Jack Ma at the Viva Tech conference in Paris, May 16, 2019*

83. "It's not easy to operate a company like Alibaba, but I'm pretty sure – I'm 100% sure – Daniel Zhang will do a better job than I do."

*—Nikkei Asian Review, May 15, 2019*

84. "Everything we innovate is to enable others to succeed – to make it easy for small businesses to do business."

*—Jack Ma at the Viva Tech conference in Paris, May 16, 2019*

# Dreams that Change the World

85. "We are never in a lack of money. We lack people with dreams who can die for those dreams."

*—Republic World, September 10, 2019*

86. "It's the dreams that keep us working hard. It's the dreams that keep us never afraid of the mistakes, the setbacks we have."

*—Alizila.com*

87. "I believe it's not the technology that changes the world. It's the dreams behind the technology that change the world."

*—YourStory.com, November 17, 2019*

88. "A lot of companies, I learned why they fail. Because they want the next quarter. They want revenues, they want profits. They forget about dreams. It's important that Alibaba dreams."

*—Financial Times, September 10, 2019*

## Investing in China

89. "In China, because of problems in water, air and food safety, in 10 or 20 years we will face a lot of health problems, like increased cancer. So that is one area where I will invest my money and time. My second focus is people's culture and education."

—*The Financial Times, December 12, 2013*

90. "I don't want people in China to have deep pockets but shallow minds."

—*Entrepreneur, October 31, 2018*

91. "We've been poor for so many years: When we made money, we put it in the banks because someday we know that disaster is coming so we can spend the money. When the economy is bad, we still have the money to spend – you guys probably don't, you worry."

—*Jack Ma at the Clinton Global Initiative meeting in New York City, September 29, 2015*

92. "China is opening, opening the door. And the Internet is the best way to let people understand what's happening outside."

—*Business Insider, June 20, 2019*

93. "People say, 'Well, you know the economy is bad, so China consumption will be low.' No, totally different. You Americans love to spend tomorrow's money, and other people's money maybe.... We Chinese love to save money."

—*Jack Ma at the Clinton Global Initiative meeting in New York City, September 29, 2015*

94. "When we export, we have a terrible sky, we have terrible water, we have a terrible environment. When we start to import, we're going to be better. So that's all a great opportunity, guys, be happy about that."

—*CNBC, September 30, 2015*

95. "China's government is so strong on investment, so strong on exporting, but they're too weak on domestic consumption. It's now the private sector's time to shine....

In the past 20 years, the government is so strong, now they're getting weak. It's our opportunity, it's our showtime to see ... how we can develop real consumption here."

—*Jack Ma at the Clinton Global Initiative meeting in New York City, September 29, 2015*

96. "China has a great culture of charity, but China needs to build up the culture of philanthropy."

—*Forbes, December 2, 2019*

97. "In China today, we have 18 [million] new babies born every year, which is not enough. We need to have much more than that. I think the best resources of the human beings or the best resources on the earth are not the coal, not the oil, not the electricity. It's the human brains."

*—Jack Ma at the World AI Conference in Shanghai, August 29, 2019*

98. "I believe China one day [will have] hundreds of thousands of business people who will build up their own charities or philanthropy foundations."

*—Jack Ma at the Forbes Global CEO Conference in Singapore, October 15, 2019*

99. "There's no country like China in the world. With political stability, social safety and 6 percent-plus economic growth, we have the best business environment."

*—The New York Times, September 7, 2018*

## Supporting Young People

100. "Help young people. Help small guys. Because small guys will be big. Young people will have the seeds you bury in their minds, and when they grow up, they will change the world."

*—Time, September 23, 2014*

101. "Hire as many young people as possible because they are never scared. We make wrong decisions, we make the wrong policies, we kill their future. So trust young people. Trust the small business. Build [an] environment, build the ecosystem for them. This is our future."

*—Tech in Asia, October 19, 2017*

102. "If young people have awe for the future, act conscientiously towards the present, and be thankful for the past, they will have opportunities."

*—YourStory.com, November 17, 2019*

103. "Having been trained as a teacher, I feel extremely proud of what I have achieved. Teachers always want their students to exceed them, so the responsible thing to do for me and the company to do is to let younger, more talented people take over in leadership roles."

*—Barron's, September 10, 2018*

# The Impact of Technology

104. "I'm not involved in technology. I'm involved in entrepreneurship.... The only thing I can use my computer is to send and receive email and browse."

—*Tech Times, 12 April, 2018*

105. "I'm a believer that technology is great for human beings."

—*YourStory.com, November 17, 2019*

106. "We are very lucky because the world is in a big transformation because of technology. This new technology will create a lot of successful people, interesting careers, but, honestly, every new technology will create social problems."

—*Jack Ma at the World Economic Forum in Davos, January 24, 2018*

107. "If we don't align together, human beings are going to fight each other, because each technological revolution makes the world unbalanced."

—*Jack Ma at the World Economic Forum in Davos, January 24, 2018*

108. "I'm not a tech guy. I'm looking at the technology with the eyes of my customers, normal people's eyes."

—*The New York Times, January 5, 2007*

109. "The biggest difference between the new century and the old lies in the difference between the eras of information technology and data technology. Information technology aims to control, while data technology aims to share,"

—*South China Morning Post, December 3, 2016*

110. "Even today, I still don't understand what coding is all about. I still don't understand the technology behind the Internet."

—*Business Insider, April 14, 2016*

# Inspiring Philanthropy

111. "We can discover and help more Jack Mas, more Bill Gates, more Warren Buffetts…"

*—Forbes, December 2, 2019*

112. "Philanthropy is not about helping others, it's about helping yourself. When you change, the world changes."

*—Business Insider, June 20, 2019*

113. "To do philanthropy well, you need to use commercial means. While bearing a philanthropic heart, do not use philanthropic means and bear a commercial heart."

*—YourStory.com, November 17, 2019*

114. "Philanthropy is also about efficiency. If you can spend $3, why spend $5? If you can finish it in two hours, why do four hours? The way I learned how to run a company, that is the way I learned how to run a philanthropic organization."

*—Forbes, December 2, 2019*

115. "The world won't change because you donate money, but it will change if your heart is changed. You can never save all the poor people and heal all the illness, but we can wake up the kindness inside everyone in the world."

—*Jack Ma at the Xin Philanthropy Conference in Hangzhou, July 25, 2016*

# Artificial Intelligence

116. "Artificial Intelligence is not a threat to humans."

*—Republic World, September 10, 2019*

117. "Artificial Intelligence should support human beings. Technology should always do something that enables people, not disables people."

*—Jack Ma at the World Economic Forum in Davos, January 24, 2018*

118. "The computer will always be smarter than you are. They never forget, they never get angry. But computers can never be as wise a man. AI and robots are going to kill a lot of jobs because, in the future, it'll be done by machines. Service industries offer hope, but they must be done uniquely."

*—Jack Ma at the World Economic Forum in Davos, January 24, 2018*

119. "Humans cannot survive without the Earth, but the Earth can survive without humans. After the industrial revolution, mankind is able to look out from the Earth, land on the Moon, establish space stations and survive in outer space.

Many great people started to explore the world outside the Earth. Mankind has huge rights, but nature can 'lay us off' at any time. Mankind should learn to coexist with nature.

A slowing down of growth in the economy is acceptable, but the growth of mankind is a must. I think AI should be translated as machine intelligence. The words we use, 'Artificial Intelligence', come from thinking too highly of mankind. Many things are very hard for humans but far easier for machines."

—*Jack Ma at the World Artificial Intelligence Conference in Shanghai, July 9, 2020*

120. "In 30 years, a robot will likely be on the cover of Time Magazine as the best CEO. Robots are quicker and more rational than humans. They don't get bogged down in emotions – like getting angry at competitors.

Machines will do what human beings are incapable of doing. Machines will partner and cooperate with humans, rather than become mankind's biggest enemy."

—*CNN Business, April 24, 2017*

121. "If machines can do things better, we have to change the way we teach. The key things are value, believing, independent thinking, teamwork, care for others, making sure humans are different from machines."

—*Business Insider, June 20, 2019*

## The Internet & E-commerce

122. "In other countries, e-commerce is a way to shop; in China it is a lifestyle."

—Duncan Clark, *Alibaba: The House That Jack Ma Built*, 2016

123. "EBay is a shark in the ocean; we are a crocodile in the Yangtze River. If we fight in the ocean, we will lose, but if we fight in the river, we will win."

—*Bloomberg*, November 9, 2014

124. "In carrying out e-commerce, the most important thing is to keep doing what you are doing right now with passion, to keep it up."

—*Business Insider*, July 1, 2016

125. "Right now there is a prime opportunity for all of us to change the rules of the game through e-commerce and shift the balance in favor of entrepreneurs like you. The Internet levels the playing field and gives everyone – be they big or small – a chance."

—Laurel J. Delaney, *Exporting: The Definitive Guide to Selling Abroad Profitably*, 2013

126. "Talking about manufacturing, we should not be talking 'Made in China,' 'Made in America.' It's going to be made in Internet."

*—Jack Ma at the Bloomberg Global Business Forum in New York, September 20, 2017*

127. "Just as the Internet is revolutionizing retail, we at Alibaba believe it will eventually do the same to fundamentally information-driven industries such as finance, education and healthcare. Once this change happens – once we are all connected – I believe the spirit of equality and transparency at the heart of the Internet will make it possible for Chinese society to leapfrog in its development of a stronger institutional and social infrastructure....

Our water has become undrinkable, our food inedible, our milk poisonous and worst of all the air in our cities is so polluted that we often cannot see the sun. Twenty years ago, people in China were focusing on economic survival. Now, people have better living conditions and big dreams for the future. But these dreams will be hollow if we cannot see the sun."

*—The Financial Times, December 12, 2013*

# How to Change the Future

128. "China changed because of us in the past fifteen years. We hope in the next fifteen years, the world changes because of us."

—Duncan Clark, Alibaba: The House That Jack Ma Built, 2016

129. "In the next three decades, the world will experience far more pain than happiness."

—CNN Business, April 24, 2017

130. "There is very little we can do to change yesterday, very little we can do to change today, but if we do a little bit today we can change the future."

—Jack Ma at the Viva Tech conference in Paris, May 16, 2019

131. "In the past decade, we measured ourselves by how much we changed China. In the future, we will be judged by how much progress we bring to the world."

—Bloomberg, November 9, 2014

132. "Do invest in the people, in the future, in small and medium-sized enterprises."

—The Kyiv Post, November 8, 2019

133. "The next 30 years are going to be critical for the world. Make the technology inclusive, make the world change. Pay attention to those people who are 30 years old. Those are the internet generation. They will change the world."

—*Business Insider, June 20, 2019*

134. "Globalization cannot be stopped. No one can stop globalization, no one can stop trade. If trade stops, the world stops. Trade is the way to dissolve the war not cause the war.

Global trade must be simple and modernized; it must be inclusive so everyone has the same opportunity. The next generation of globalization must be inclusive."

—*Jack Ma at the World Economic Forum in Davos, January 24, 2018*

135. "The finance industry needs disrupters, it needs outsiders to come in and carry out a transformation."

—*Duncan Clark, Alibaba: The House That Jack Ma Built, 2016*

136. "If people criticize you, you have to think. And I spent most of my time thinking about the future. I spend most of my time listening to the complaints.

Because people like me, we don't have money, we don't have the technology, we don't have a strong relationship, the only thing we compete with the others is that how we see the future."

—*CNBC, June 4, 2019*

137. "People in China and America, one thing we have in common is the heart of love and respect. This is a common language we have. The first tech revolution caused WWI, the second caused WWII, now we are a third revolution, what's gonna happen? It should be a war against poverty, disease, etc."

—*Bloomberg, September 7, 2018*

138. "In 10 or 20 years, people will work less than four hours a day, maybe three days a week. With less time spent working, we will question how to live."

—*CNN Business, April 24, 2017*

# Part 3: SUCCESS LESSONS

## Put Customers First

139. "Let the Wall Street investors curse us if they wish. We will still follow the principle of customers first, employees second and investors third."

*—Bloomberg, November 9, 2014*

140. "Putting the shareholders first is capitalism's biggest mistake. Shareholders do not have a long-term vision for the company."

*—Bloomberg, November 9, 2014*

141. "Forget about your competitors. Just focus on your customers."

*—YourStory.com, November 17, 2019*

142. "If the customer loves you, the government will have to love you."

*—YourStory.com, November 17, 2019*

143. "If your customer is happy and employee is happy, then shareholders will also be happy. Think this is a pipedream? Think again."

*—Jack Ma at Gateway '17 in Detroit, June 21, 2017*

144. "You've to make consumers smart. An e-commerce portal doesn't sell a product at cheaper rates. Instead, an offline shop sells it at a costlier price."

—*YourStory.com, November 17, 2019*

145. "Spend time on your customers, on your people, on your teams. Don't spend time on your competitors or investors. When you spend time on the people you serve, when they're happy – you win! That's the very simple."

—*Jack Ma at the Viva Tech conference in Paris, May 16, 2019*

## Choose to be Optimistic

146. "As entrepreneurs, if you're not optimistic, you're in trouble. So the people I choose, they have to be optimistic."

> —*Jack Ma at the annual meeting with IMF and World Bank in Indonesia, October 12, 2018*

147. "The best people are optimistic and don't complain."

> —*Jack Ma at the World Economic Forum in Davos, January 23, 2019*

## Never Give Up

148. "Never give up. Today is hard, tomorrow will be worse, but the day after tomorrow will be sunshine."

—*Republic World, September 10, 2019*

149. "Giving up is the greatest failure."

—*The Economic Times, September 25, 2014*

150. "Today is difficult, tomorrow is much more difficult, but the day after tomorrow is beautiful. Most people die tomorrow evening."

—*Business Insider, June 20, 2019*

151. "If you don't put out more time and energy than others, how can you achieve the success you want?"

—*YourStory.com, November 17, 2019*

152. "Be the last man standing."

—*Duncan Clark, Alibaba: The House That Jack Ma Built, 2016*

153. "Always keep in mind these three principles: what you want to do, what you should do, and for how long you should do it."

—*Jack Ma at the Beijing Network Operators Meeting, March 17, 2008*

154. "If you want to be successful tomorrow, it's impossible. If you want to be successful a year later, it's impossible. But if you want to win 10 years later, you have a chance."

*—Business Insider, June 20, 2019*

155. "We will make it because we are young and we will never, never give up."

*—Business Insider, July 1, 2016*

# Hire Smart People

156. "My job is to make sure smart people can work together. Stupid people can work together easily, smart people can't."

*—Jack Ma at the World Economic Forum in Davos, January 24, 2018*

157. "Hire the person best suited to the job, not the most talented. That can be a very painful lesson. There's no point putting in a Boeing jet engine when you need to run a tractor."

*—Business Insider, July 1, 2016*

158. "If we are a good team and know what we want to do, one of us can defeat 10 of them."

*—The Economic Times, September 25, 2014*

159. "Intelligent people need a fool to lead them. When the team's all a bunch of scientists, it is best to have a peasant lead the way. His way of thinking is different. It's easier to win if you have people seeing things from different perspectives."

*—Business Insider, June 20, 2019*

160. "You need the right people with you, not the best people."

*—Republic World, September 10, 2019*

161. "At first, I knew nothing about technology. I knew nothing about management. But you don't have to know a lot of things. You have to find people who are smarter than you are."

—*Inc. Magazine, February 15, 2018*

# Learn from Other People's Mistakes

162. "If you want to be successful, learn from other people's mistakes, not their successes."

—*Business Insider, June 20, 2019*

163. "No matter how smart you are, you will encounter mistakes. You learn from from other people's mistakes not because you will be able to avoid mistakes when they come, [when] these suffers come. You'll learn how to deal with it, how to face it."

—*Jack Ma at the World Economic Forum in Davos, January 24, 2018*

164. "In life, it's not how much we achieved, it's how much we've gone through the tough days and mistakes."

—*CNBC, January 30, 2018*

## Leaders Never Complain

165. "Leadership is your instinct, then it's your training. Leaders are always positive, they never complain."

*—Business Insider, June 20, 2019*

166. "A leader should have higher grit and tenacity, and be able to endure what the employees can't."

*—Entrepreneur, October 31, 2018*

167. "A good boss is better than a good company."

*—Jack Ma's speech at De La Salle University, October 25, 2017*

168. "A leader should never compare his technical skills with his employees."

*—Republic World, September 10, 2019*

169. "A leader should incentivize but not with money. You give trust, respect, appreciation, and correct, heartfelt advice."

*—Jack Ma at the World Economic Forum in Davos, January 24, 2018*

170. "When people think too highly of you, you have the responsibility to calm down and be yourself."

*—YourStory.com, November 17, 2019*

171. "For a leader, vision, heart, and strength are the most important. All these years, I've continuously upheld this belief.

Leaders cannot be unable to broaden their vision; when we compete with others, we're competing to see who can see the furthest, the loftiest. It's becoming more and more difficult to do business. The further your vision can stretch, the farther your journey must be."

—*Vulcan Post, May 22, 2015*

## Focus on Making Values

172. "I do everything to make sure my customer is happy, my employee is happy, society is healthy. I would focus on customers, I would focus on not making money, I would focus on making values."

*—Business Insider, June 20, 2019*

173. "All the business people would say, 'Jack, what are you busy with now?' I said, 'I'm busy with building the value system.' They said, 'Jack, you're so stupid. 99 percent of business in China doesn't care about that. What they care about is making money. Making money is the business, making money is the value.'

And I don't believe that. I think making money is the result, making money is not the goal. Your goal is to change, influence the world and improve the country."

*—Talk Asia, CNN, April 25, 2006*

## Don't Worry

174. "If you think the technology revolution is a problem, I'm sorry to say a problem just started. If you think it's an opportunity, the opportunity just started. The only thing is your mentality. If the mentality is now a worry, you'll worry all the time."

*—Jack Ma at the Viva Tech conference in Paris, May 16, 2019*

175. "American people worry too much about the China economy. Every time you think China is a problem, we get better, but when you have a high expectation for China, China is always a problem."

*—CNBC, September 30, 2015*

176. "In business, never worry about competition, never worry about the pressure. If you worry about pressure, don't be a businessman…. If you create value, there is an opportunity. Today the whole world worries. That means there is a great opportunity."

*—Jack Ma at the World Economic Forum in Davos, January 23, 2019*

# Part 4: BRILLIANT ADVICE FOR ENTREPRENEURS

## How to Build a Successful Company

177. "To manage smart people, you have to use culture, the value system they believe what they do. If you just want to use rules and laws and documents to control – that's how you control stupid people."

—*Jack Ma at the World Economic Forum in Davos, January 23, 2019*

178. "Players should never fight. A real businessman or entrepreneur has no enemies. Once he understands this, the sky's the limit."

—*Jack Ma's speech at De La Salle University, October 25, 2017*

179. "The best way to promote your company is through your product or services, or employees."

—*Jack Ma at the World Economic Forum in Davos, January 24, 2018*

180. "You should learn from your competitor but never copy. Copy, and you die."

—*YourStory.com, November 17, 2019*

181. "We strove for bigger and stronger companies in the last century. Today we need to think how to create good companies. We need to make our clients, society, employees, ourselves and our families happy. Only good companies like this can last."

—*The New York Times, September 10, 2019*

182. "Focus is essential for business. When laying down the strategic goals for your business, you must never exceed three. Once you've exceeded three, you won't be able to remember them, and neither will your workers. When you set down goals each year, just determine the three most important, and cut out the fourth.

Why is Alibaba a seven-company business, rather than eight? A person's management capabilities have limits; one can only manage at most seven teams. Seven and below will pose no problem, [but] exceeding that will definitely bring about problems. In terms of small startups, the strategic thing to do is to survive."

—*Vulcan Post, May 22, 2015*

183. "Never, ever do business with government. Love them. Don't marry them."

—*CNN Business, September 9, 2018*

## Failure & Patience

184. "It doesn't matter if I failed. At least I passed the concept on to others. Even if I don't succeed, someone will succeed."

*—The Economic Times, September 25, 2014*

185. "You have got to keep trying, and if it doesn't work, you always can revert back to what you were doing before."

*—YourStory.com, November 17, 2019*

186. "The very important thing you should have is patience."

*—Medium, September 12, 2019*

187. "I think everybody can be successful if you really try hard."

*—Jack Ma at the Viva Tech conference in Paris, May 16, 2019*

## Opportunities for Business Growth

188. "Opportunity lies in the place where the complaints are."

*—Entrepreneur, October 31, 2018*

189. "If you want to grow, find a good opportunity. Today, if you want to be a great company, think about what social problem you could solve."

*—Business Insider, July 1, 2016*

190. "The opportunities that everyone cannot see are the real opportunities."

*—YourStory.com, November 17, 2019*

191. "In the past thirty years, USA domestic consumption was the engine of the global economy. And I told people at that time, if you miss the opportunity of selling your products to the world, to the USA, to Europe, you might miss the chance.

Today I want to tell people that if you miss the opportunity of selling your products to China, you will miss the future."

*—Quartz, June 19, 2017*

## Women in Business

192. "If you want your company to be successful, if you want your company to operate with wisdom, with care, then women are the best."

—*Jack Ma's interview for World Economic Forum 2018, January 24, 2018*

193. "The secret sauce of Alibaba's success is that 34% of the senior leadership of Alibaba are women, and almost 47% of employees are women.

I have a lot of powerful women standing behind me, and I'm always thankful for them."

—*Forbes, December 2, 2019*

194. "In the age of AI, women's attention to experience and detail can outperform machine learning, whereas men's traits of rational thinking will be challenged by machines."

—*YourStory.com, November 17, 2019*

195. "I believe I can do better in 3 areas: supporting entrepreneurs, education and fighting for more women leaders."

—*Jack Ma at the Viva Tech conference in Paris, May 16, 2019*

# Productivity Tips for Entrepreneurs

196. "When I went to Las Vegas, my gambling limit was $500. I like to play cards. I'm not very good, because I don't want to calculate. I just play by instinct. But I've learned a lot of business philosophy by playing poker."

*—The New York Times, January 5, 2007*

197. "Of course, you're not happy when people say, 'No.' Have a good sleep, wake up, and try again."

*—Jack Ma at the Viva Tech conference in Paris, May 16, 2019*

198. "If there are nine rabbits on the ground, if you want to catch one, just focus on one. Change your tactics if you need to but don't change the rabbit.... Get one first, put it in your pocket, and then catch the others."

*—Business Insider, April 14, 2016*

199. "When you are 20 to 30 years old, you should follow a good boss [and] join a good company to learn how to do things properly. When you are 30 to 40 years old, if you want to do something yourself, just do it. You still can afford to lose, to fail.

When you are 40-50 years old, just focus on the things you are good at. When you are 50 to 60 years old, spend time training and developing young people, the next generation. When you're over 60 years old, spend time with your grandchildren. Enjoy yourself, right? That's the life."

*—Jack Ma at the World Economic Forum in Davos, January 23, 2019*

# 7 Book Recommendations from Jack Ma

1. A Hero Born by Jin Yong
2. Tao Te Ching: A Book About the Way and the Power of the Way by Lao Tzu
3. Built to Last: Successful Habits of Visionary Companies by Jim Collins and Jerry I. Porras
1. 4 The Long Tail: Why the Future of Business Is Selling Less of More Kindle Edition by Chris Anderson
4. Here Comes Everybody: The Power of Organizing Without Organizations by Clay Shirky
5. Business Cycles: A Theoretical, Historical, And Statistical Analysis of the Capitalist Process by Joseph Alois Schumpeter
6. Makers: The New Industrial Revolution by Chris Anderson

Scan the QR Code to find more information for each book.

## FREE book

For a limited time, Olivia Longray is giving away the book called "A Simple Weight Loss Plan That Can Work for You: How to Lose Weight Quickly in an Atmosphere of Love."

This is your only chance to get it FREE (no strings attached).

Scan this QR code.

Enjoy!

## Your Reviews

If the book proves useful and appealing to you, please, leave a short review on the book's Amazon page and give me your thoughts on it! Your opinion will surely help other readers to decide if my book is worth their time and money. Tell others of your impressions and my thanks to you for it in advance!

Have a great day!

Olivia Longray

# A Note on Sources

1. James Fallows, "Could There Ever be an 'American Alibaba'? Jack Ma's Biographer Explains What It Would Take", April 16, 2016, https://www.theatlantic.com/notes/2016/04/could-there-ever-be-an-american-alibaba-his-biographer-explains-what-it-would-take/478608/
2. Zameena Mejia, "Self-made billionaire Jack Ma: How to be successful in your 20s, 30s, 40s and beyond," CNBC, January 30, 2018, https://www.cnbc.com/2018/01/30/jack-ma-dont-fear-making-mistakes-in-your-20s-and-30s.html
3. Rebecca Fannin, "How I Did It: Jack Ma, Alibaba.com. The unlikely rise of China's hottest internet tycoon," Inc., January 1, 2008, https://www.inc.com/magazine/20080101/how-i-did-it-jack-ma-alibaba.html
4. Frederick E. Allen, "What Makes Alibaba's Jack Ma a Great Innovator?" Forbes, May 7, 2014, https://www.forbes.com/sites/frederickallen/2014/05/07/what-makes-jack-ma-a-great-innovator/#3a5dcf582c71
5. Rebecca Fannin, "How I Did It: Jack Ma, Alibaba.com. The unlikely rise of China's hottest internet tycoon," Inc., January 1, 2008, https://www.inc.com/magazine/20080101/how-i-did-it-jack-ma-alibaba.html
6. Sonia Kolesnikov-Jessop, "Spotlight: Jack Ma, co-founder of Alibaba.com - Business - International Herald Tribune," The New York Times, January 5, 2007, https://www.nytimes.com/2007/01/05/business/worldbusiness/05iht-wbspot06.4109874.html
7. Sonia Kolesnikov-Jessop, "Spotlight: Jack Ma, co-founder of Alibaba.com - Business - International Herald Tribune," The New York Times, January 5, 2007, https://www.nytimes.com/2007/01/05/business/worldbusiness/05iht-wbspot06.4109874.html
8. "Do sleep, don't have doubts. Jack Ma's guide to sanity and success," World Economic Forum, January 23, 2019, https://wef.ch/2R9983S

9. Pilita Clark, "Billionaires should be seen and not heard," Financial Times, February 3, 2019, https://www.ft.com/content/70836020-253a-11e9-8ce6-5db4543da632

10. Catherine Clifford, "Alibaba billionaire Jack Ma: Almost 'everybody can be successful if you really try hard,'" CNBC.com, June 4, 2019, https://www.cnbc.com/2019/06/04/alibabas-jack-ma-almost-everyone-can-be-successful.html

11. Rebecca Fannin, "How I Did It: Jack Ma, Alibaba.com. The unlikely rise of China's hottest internet tycoon," Inc., January 1, 2008, https://www.inc.com/magazine/20080101/how-i-did-it-jack-ma-alibaba.html

12. "Jack Ma on the IQ of love - and other top quotes from his Davos interview," World Economic Forum, January 24, 2018, https://www.weforum.org/agenda/2018/01/jack-ma-davos-top-quotes/

13. "Jack Ma: China's controversial 'Mr. Internet,'" Deutsche Welle, , September 10, 2014, https://www.dw.com/en/jack-ma-chinas-controversial-mr-internet/a-17912243

14. William Mellor, Lulu Yilun Chen, Zijing Wu, "Ma Says Alibaba Shareholders Should Feel Love, Not No. 3," Bloomberg, November 9, 2014, https://www.bloomberg.com/news/articles/2014-11-09/ma-says-alibaba-shareholders-should-feel-love-not-no-3

15. "Do sleep, don't have doubts. Jack Ma's guide to sanity and success," World Economic Forum, January 23, 2019, https://wef.ch/2R9983S

16. Rebecca Fannin, "How I Did It: Jack Ma, Alibaba.com. The unlikely rise of China's hottest internet tycoon," Inc., January 1, 2008, https://www.inc.com/magazine/20080101/how-i-did-it-jack-ma-alibaba.html

17. Charlie Rose, "Charlie Rose Talks to Alibaba's Jack Ma," Bloomberg Businessweek, January 30, 2015, https://www.bloomberg.com/news/articles/2015-01-29/alibaba-s-jack-ma-on-early-obstacles-his-ambitions

18. "Future of work: 5 top insights from Davos experts World Economic Forum," World Economic Forum, 25 January, 2019, https://www.weforum.org/agenda/2019/01/future-of-work-tk-top-trends-from-davos/

19. Rebecca Fannin, "How I Did It: Jack Ma, Alibaba.com. The unlikely rise of China's hottest internet tycoon," Inc., January 1, 2008, https://www.inc.com/magazine/20080101/how-i-did-it-jack-ma-alibaba.html

20. "Interview Jack Ma – Alibaba.com," Talk Asia, CNN, April 25, 2006, https://edition.cnn.com/2006/WORLD/asiapcf/04/24/talkasia.ma.script/

21. Rebecca Fannin, "How I Did It: Jack Ma, Alibaba.com. The unlikely rise of China's hottest internet tycoon," Inc., January 1, 2008, https://www.inc.com/magazine/20080101/how-i-did-it-jack-ma-alibaba.html

22. Jackie Wattles, "How Jack Ma went from English teacher to tech billionaire," CNN Business, September 9, 2018, https://money.cnn.com/2018/09/09/technology/business/jack-ma-alibaba-bio/index.html

23. Rebecca Fannin, "How I Did It: Jack Ma, Alibaba.com. The unlikely rise of China's hottest internet tycoon," Inc., January 1, 2008, https://www.inc.com/magazine/20080101/how-i-did-it-jack-ma-alibaba.html

24. Rebecca Fannin, "How I Did It: Jack Ma, Alibaba.com. The unlikely rise of China's hottest internet tycoon," Inc., January 1, 2008, https://www.inc.com/magazine/20080101/how-i-did-it-jack-ma-alibaba.html

25. Tom Brennan, "At Viva Tech, Jack Ma urges using tech for good," Alizila.com, May 16, 2019, https://www.alizila.com/at-viva-tech-jack-ma-urges-using-tech-for-good/

26. Rebecca Fannin, "How I Did It: Jack Ma, Alibaba.com. The unlikely rise of China's hottest internet tycoon," Inc., January 1, 2008,

https://www.inc.com/magazine/20080101/how-i-did-it-jack-ma-alibaba.html

27. Charlie Rose, "Charlie Rose Talks to Alibaba's Jack Ma," Bloomberg Businesweek, January 30, 2015, https://www.bloomberg.com/news/articles/2015-01-29/alibaba-s-jack-ma-on-early-obstacles-his-ambitions

28. Rahul R, "Jack Ma Steps Down From Alibaba: His Quotes On AI, Life Are Unmissable," Republic World, September 10, 2019, https://www.republicworld.com/technology-news/apps/jack-ma-steps-down-from-alibaba-his-quotes-on-ai-life-are-unmissable.html

29. Sampath Putrevu, "38 quotes by Jack Ma on work, technology, women, and philanthropy," YourStory.com, November 17, 2019, https://yourstory.com/2019/11/jack-ma-quotes-alibaba-singles-day

30. Justin Doebele, "Jack Ma Outlines Bold Vision For His Philanthropy Foundation," Forbes, December 2, 2019, https://www.forbes.com/sites/jdoebele/2019/12/02/jack-ma-shares-his-plans-for-education-philanthropy-in-china/#2b1a8e915c7f

31. Jack Linshi, "5 Life Lessons From Alibaba Founder Jack Ma," Time, September 23, 2014, https://time.com/3423708/5-life-lessons-jack-ma-alibaba/

32. Sampath Putrevu, "38 quotes by Jack Ma on work, technology, women, and philanthropy," YourStory.com, November 17, 2019, https://yourstory.com/2019/11/jack-ma-quotes-alibaba-singles-day

33. Kana Inagaki, "Too much money leads to 'a lot of mistakes', says Jack Ma," Financial Times, December 6 2019, https://www.ft.com/content/8a9847dc-180a-11ea-9ee4-11f260415385

34. Sampath Putrevu, "38 quotes by Jack Ma on work, technology, women, and philanthropy," YourStory.com, November 17, 2019, https://yourstory.com/2019/11/jack-ma-quotes-alibaba-singles-day

35. Caroline Frost, "Jack Ma, the richest man in China, stepped down as Alibaba chairman — here are 27 of his most brilliant quotes," Business Insider, June 20, 2019,

https://markets.businessinsider.com/news/stocks/jack-ma-quotes-alibaba-inspirational-2019-6-1028295089#-a-leader-should-incentivize-but-not-with-money-you-give-trust-respect-appreciation-and-correct-heartfelt-advice-3

36. Jolene Hee, "'We Were Actually Very Silly': Billionaire Jack Ma On Success, Luck & Speaking Harsh Truths," Vulcan Post, May 22, 2015, https://vulcanpost.com/246691/jack-ma-success-luck-speaking-harsh-truths/

37. Jack Linshi, "5 Life Lessons From Alibaba Founder Jack Ma," Time, September 23, 2014, https://time.com/3423708/5-life-lessons-jack-ma-alibaba/

38. "Alibaba's Ma Reflects On 12-Year Journey at China 2.0 Conference," Stanford Graduate School of Business, June 19, 2013, https://www.youtube.com/watch?v=euxJhgYZXL8

39. Jolene Hee, "'We Were Actually Very Silly': Billionaire Jack Ma On Success, Luck & Speaking Harsh Truths," Vulcan Post, May 22, 2015, https://vulcanpost.com/246691/jack-ma-success-luck-speaking-harsh-truths/

40. Sampath Putrevu, "38 quotes by Jack Ma on work, technology, women, and philanthropy," YourStory.com, November 17, 2019, https://yourstory.com/2019/11/jack-ma-quotes-alibaba-singles-day

41. Bhavya Kaushal, "Know the Tricks of the Trade from the Undisputed King of Business: Jack Ma," Entrepreneur, October 31, 2018, https://www.entrepreneur.com/slideshow/322603

42. Sampath Putrevu, "38 quotes by Jack Ma on work, technology, women, and philanthropy," YourStory.com, November 17, 2019, https://yourstory.com/2019/11/jack-ma-quotes-alibaba-singles-day

43. Caroline Frost, "Jack Ma, the richest man in China, stepped down as Alibaba chairman — here are 27 of his most brilliant quotes," Business Insider, June 20, 2019, https://markets.businessinsider.com/news/stocks/jack-ma-quotes-alibaba-inspirational-2019-6-1028295089#-a-leader-should-incentivize-but-not-with-money-you-give-trust-respect-appreciation-and-correct-heartfelt-advice-3

44. Wilson Lee Flores, "Life & success secrets of the humble billionaire Jack Ma," The Philippine Star, October 28, 2017, https://www.philstar.com/lifestyle/sunday-life/2017/10/28/1753386/life-success-secrets-humble-billionaire-jack-ma

45. Davide Scialpi, "JACK MA's quotes about Success and Leadership — Founder of ALIBABA Group — selected by Davide Scialpi," Medium, May 17, 2018, https://medium.com/@davidescialpi/jack-mas-quotes-about-success-and-leadership-founder-of-alibaba-group-9fea5577f12

46. Jack Linshi, "5 Life Lessons From Alibaba Founder Jack Ma," Time, September 23, 2014, https://time.com/3423708/5-life-lessons-jack-ma-alibaba/

47. James Fallows, "Could There Ever be an 'American Alibaba'? Jack Ma's Biographer Explains What It Would Take", April 16, 2016, https://www.theatlantic.com/notes/2016/04/could-there-ever-be-an-american-alibaba-his-biographer-explains-what-it-would-take/478608/

48. Jolene Hee, "'We Were Actually Very Silly': Billionaire Jack Ma On Success, Luck & Speaking Harsh Truths," Vulcan Post, May 22, 2015, https://vulcanpost.com/246691/jack-ma-success-luck-speaking-harsh-truths/

49. "Jack Ma on the IQ of love - and other top quotes from his Davos interview," World Economic Forum, January 24, 2018, https://www.weforum.org/agenda/2018/01/jack-ma-davos-top-quotes/

50. Tara Law, "Davos Daily Review: Angela Merkel, New Zealand's Jacinda Ardern and Alibaba's Jack Ma," Time, January 23, 2019, https://time.com/collection/davos-2019/5511150/davos-day-2-merkel-ardern-ma/

51. Davide Scialpi, "JACK MA's quotes about Success and Leadership — Founder of ALIBABA Group — selected by Davide Scialpi," Medium, May 17, 2018, https://medium.com/@davidescialpi/jack-mas-quotes-about-success-and-leadership-founder-of-alibaba-group-9fea5577f12

52. Duncan Clark, "How self-made billionaire Jack Ma used charisma and masterful speaking skills to build the Alibaba empire," April 14, 2016, https://www.businessinsider.com/the-billionaire-founder-of-alibaba-has-been-giving-a-similar-speech-for-17-years-heres-how-he-always-engages-his-audience-2016-4

53. Verne G. Kopytoff, "Jack Ma Wants a Smaller Yahoo," Sarasota Herald-Tribune, June 2, 2011, https://www.heraldtribune.com/article/LK/20110602/News/605199699/SH?template=ampart

54. John Smith, "10 Best Motivational Quotes on Success by Jack MA," Medium, September 12, 2019, https://medium.com/@videomonk75/10-best-motivational-quotes-on-success-by-jack-ma-814c6df15e35

55. Jillian D'Onfro, "15 quotes that show the strange, relentless genius of billionaire Alibaba founder Jack Ma," July 1, 2016, https://www.businessinsider.com/alibaba-founder-jack-ma-quotes-2016-6

56. Jolene Hee, "'We Were Actually Very Silly': Billionaire Jack Ma On Success, Luck & Speaking Harsh Truths," Vulcan Post, May 22, 2015, https://vulcanpost.com/246691/jack-ma-success-luck-speaking-harsh-truths/

57. Jolene Hee, "'We Were Actually Very Silly': Billionaire Jack Ma On Success, Luck & Speaking Harsh Truths," Vulcan Post, May 22, 2015, https://vulcanpost.com/246691/jack-ma-success-luck-speaking-harsh-truths/

58. Eva Dou, "Jack Ma Says Fakes "Better Quality and Better Price Than the Real Names," The Wall Street Journal, June 15, 2016, https://blogs.wsj.com/chinarealtime/2016/06/15/jack-ma-says-fakes-better-quality-and-better-price-than-the-real-names/

59. Jillian D'Onfro, "15 quotes that show the strange, relentless genius of billionaire Alibaba founder Jack Ma," July 1, 2016, https://www.businessinsider.com/alibaba-founder-jack-ma-quotes-2016-6

60. Verne G. Kopytoff, "Jack Ma Wants a Smaller Yahoo," Sarasota Herald-Tribune, June 2, 2011,

https://www.heraldtribune.com/article/LK/20110602/News/605199699/SH?template=ampart

61. Rebecca Fannin, "How I Did It: Jack Ma, Alibaba.com. The unlikely rise of China's hottest internet tycoon," Inc., January 1, 2008, https://www.inc.com/magazine/20080101/how-i-did-it-jack-ma-alibaba.html

62. Caroline Frost, "Jack Ma, the richest man in China, stepped down as Alibaba chairman — here are 27 of his most brilliant quotes," Business Insider, June 20, 2019, https://markets.businessinsider.com/news/stocks/jack-ma-quotes-alibaba-inspirational-2019-6-1028295089#-a-leader-should-incentivize-but-not-with-money-you-give-trust-respect-appreciation-and-correct-heartfelt-advice-3

63. Sonia Kolesnikov-Jessop, "Spotlight: Jack Ma, co-founder of Alibaba.com - Business - International Herald Tribune," The New York Times, January 5, 2007, https://www.nytimes.com/2007/01/05/business/worldbusiness/05iht-wbspot06.4109874.html

64. "Do sleep, don't have doubts. Jack Ma's guide to sanity and success," World Economic Forum, January 23, 2019, https://wef.ch/2R9983S

65. Li Yuan, "Jack Ma Is Retiring From Alibaba. He Won't Go Far.," The New York Times, September 10, 2019, https://www.nytimes.com/2019/09/10/business/alibaba-jack-ma-retire.html

66. Rebecca Fannin, "How I Did It: Jack Ma, Alibaba.com. The unlikely rise of China's hottest internet tycoon," Inc., January 1, 2008, https://www.inc.com/magazine/20080101/how-i-did-it-jack-ma-alibaba.html

67. Isabel Togoh, "Jack Ma Marks Alibaba Retirement With Rockstar Party," Forbes, September 11, 2019, https://www.forbes.com/sites/isabeltogoh/2019/09/11/jack-ma-marks-alibaba-retirement-with-rockstar-party/#7f642e241a62

68. Tom Brennan, "At Viva Tech, Jack Ma urges using tech for good," Alizila.com, May 16, 2019,

https://www.alizila.com/at-viva-tech-jack-ma-urges-using-tech-for-good/

69. Lulu Yilun Chen, Tom Mackenzie, "Billionaire Jack Ma Prepares for Life After Alibaba," September 7, 2018, https://www.bloomberg.com/news/articles/2018-09-06/billionaire-jack-ma-prepares-for-life-after-alibaba

70. Chunying Zhang, "Elon Musk is debating Alibaba founder Jack Ma at an AI conference," Financial Review, August 29, 2019, https://www.afr.com/technology/elon-musk-is-debating-alibaba-founder-jack-ma-at-an-ai-conference-20190829-p52lvb

71. Frederick E. Allen, "What Makes Alibaba's Jack Ma a Great Innovator?", Forbes, May 7, 2014, https://www.forbes.com/sites/frederickallen/2014/05/07/what-makes-jack-ma-a-great-innovator/#3a5dcf582c71

72. Jillian D'Onfro, "15 quotes that show the strange, relentless genius of billionaire Alibaba founder Jack Ma," July 1, 2016, https://www.businessinsider.com/alibaba-founder-jack-ma-quotes-2016-6

73. "Do sleep, don't have doubts. Jack Ma's guide to sanity and success," World Economic Forum, January 23, 2019, https://wef.ch/2R9983S

74. Rebecca Fannin, "How I Did It: Jack Ma, Alibaba.com. The unlikely rise of China's hottest internet tycoon," Inc., January 1, 2008, https://www.inc.com/magazine/20080101/how-i-did-it-jack-ma-alibaba.html

75. Jillian D'Onfro, "15 quotes that show the strange, relentless genius of billionaire Alibaba founder Jack Ma," July 1, 2016, https://www.businessinsider.com/alibaba-founder-jack-ma-quotes-2016-6

76. Jack Linshi, "5 Life Lessons From Alibaba Founder Jack Ma," Time, September 23, 2014, https://time.com/3423708/5-life-lessons-jack-ma-alibaba/

77. "Jack Ma on the IQ of love - and other top quotes from his Davos interview," World Economic Forum, January 24, 2018, https://www.weforum.org/agenda/2018/01/jack-ma-davos-top-quotes/

78. Rebecca Fannin, "How I Did It: Jack Ma, Alibaba.com. The unlikely rise of China's hottest internet tycoon," Inc., January 1, 2008, https://www.inc.com/magazine/20080101/how-i-did-it-jack-ma-alibaba.html

79. Anita Balakrishnan, "Jack Ma explains the difference between Alibaba and Amazon: 'Amazon is more like an empire'," CNBC, January 18, https://www.cnbc.com/2017/01/18/jack-ma-difference-between-alibaba-and-amazon.html

80. Anita Balakrishnan, "Jack Ma explains the difference between Alibaba and Amazon: 'Amazon is more like an empire'," CNBC, January 18, https://www.cnbc.com/2017/01/18/jack-ma-difference-between-alibaba-and-amazon.html

81. "10 memorable quotes by Alibaba's Jack Ma," The Economic Times, September 25, 2014, https://economictimes.indiatimes.com/magazines/panache/10-memorable-quotes-by-alibabas-jack-ma/articleshow/43399445.cms

82. Tom Brennan, "At Viva Tech, Jack Ma urges using tech for good," Alizila.com, May 16, 2019, https://www.alizila.com/at-viva-tech-jack-ma-urges-using-tech-for-good/

83. Kenji Kawase, "After Jack: Alibaba searches for new growth in the post-Ma era," Nikkei Asian Review, May 15, 2019, https://asia.nikkei.com/Spotlight/The-Big-Story/After-Jack-Alibaba-searches-for-new-growth-in-the-post-Ma-era

84. Tom Brennan, "At Viva Tech, Jack Ma urges using tech for good," Alizila.com, May 16, 2019, https://www.alizila.com/at-viva-tech-jack-ma-urges-using-tech-for-good/

85. Rahul R, "Jack Ma Steps Down From Alibaba: His Quotes On AI, Life Are Unmissable," epublic World, September 10, 2019, https://www.republicworld.com/technology-news/apps/jack-ma-steps-down-from-alibaba-his-quotes-on-ai-life-are-unmissable.html

86. "Jack Ma Returns to Hupan: Birthplace of Alibaba," Alizila.com, https://www.alizila.com/video/return-to-hupan-birthplace-of-alibaba/

87. Sampath Putrevu, "38 quotes by Jack Ma on work, technology, women, and philanthropy," YourStory.com, November 17, 2019, https://yourstory.com/2019/11/jack-ma-quotes-alibaba-singles-day

88. Louise Lucas, "Jack Ma retires from Alibaba," Financial Times, September 10, 2019, https://www.ft.com/content/4ed760ce-d38c-11e9-8367-807ebd53ab77

89. Jamil Anderlini, "Person of the year: Jack Ma," The Financial Times, December 12, 2013, https://www.ft.com/content/308e46a8-6189-11e3-916e-00144feabdc0#axzz3139OjXpI

90. Bhavya Kaushal, "Know the Tricks of the Trade from the Undisputed King of Business: Jack Ma," Entrepreneur, October 31, 2018, https://www.entrepreneur.com/slideshow/322603

91. Everett Rosenfeld, "Jack Ma to US: Quit worrying so much about China," CNBC, September 30, 2015, https://www.cnbc.com/2015/09/30/us-quit-worrying-so-much-about-china.html

92. Caroline Frost, "Jack Ma, the richest man in China, stepped down as Alibaba chairman — here are 27 of his most brilliant quotes," Business Insider, June 20, 2019, https://markets.businessinsider.com/news/stocks/jack-ma-quotes-alibaba-inspirational-2019-6-1028295089#-a-leader-should-incentivize-but-not-with-money-you-give-trust-respect-appreciation-and-correct-heartfelt-advice-3

93. Everett Rosenfeld, "Jack Ma to US: Quit worrying so much about China," CNBC, September 30, 2015, https://www.cnbc.com/2015/09/30/us-quit-worrying-so-much-about-china.html

94. Everett Rosenfeld, "Jack Ma to US: Quit worrying so much about China," CNBC, September 30, 2015, https://www.cnbc.com/2015/09/30/us-quit-worrying-so-much-about-china.html

95. Everett Rosenfeld, "Jack Ma to US: Quit worrying so much about China," CNBC, September 30, 2015, https://www.cnbc.com/2015/09/30/us-quit-worrying-so-much-about-china.html

96. Justin Doebele, "Jack Ma Outlines Bold Vision For His Philanthropy Foundation," Forbes, December 2, 2019, https://www.forbes.com/sites/jdoebele/2019/12/02/jack-ma-shares-his-plans-for-education-philanthropy-in-china/#2b1a8e915c7f

97. Chunying Zhang, "Elon Musk is debating Alibaba founder Jack Ma at an AI conference," Financial Review, August 29, 2019, https://www.afr.com/technology/elon-musk-is-debating-alibaba-founder-jack-ma-at-an-ai-conference-20190829-p52lvb

98. Justin Doebele, "Jack Ma Outlines Bold Vision For His Philanthropy Foundation," Forbes, December 2, 2019, https://www.forbes.com/sites/jdoebele/2019/12/02/jack-ma-shares-his-plans-for-education-philanthropy-in-china/#2b1a8e915c7f

99. Li Yuan, "Alibaba's Jack Ma, China's Richest Man, to Retire From Company He Co-Founded," The New York Times, September 7, 2018, https://www.nytimes.com/2018/09/07/technology/alibaba-jack-ma-retiring.html

100. Jack Linshi, "5 Life Lessons From Alibaba Founder Jack Ma," Time, September 23, 2014, https://time.com/3423708/5-life-lessons-jack-ma-alibaba/

101. "Video: Jack Ma tells entrepreneurs 'Don't be scared'," Tech in Asia, October 19, 2017, https://www.techinasia.com/video-jack-ma-tells-entrepreneurs-dont-scared

102. Sampath Putrevu, "38 quotes by Jack Ma on work, technology, women, and philanthropy," YourStory.com, November 17, 2019, https://yourstory.com/2019/11/jack-ma-quotes-alibaba-singles-day

103. Stella Yifan Xie, "Jack Ma Is Stepping Down at Alibaba. He Was a Showman Who Showed China a New Way to Do Business," Barron's, September 10, 2018,

https://www.barrons.com/articles/jack-ma-leaving-alibaba-1536594946

104. Vincent Lanaria, "Jack Ma: 14 Amazing Facts About Alibaba's Co-Founder Tech Times," Tech Times, 12 April, 2018, https://www.techtimes.com/articles/224602/20180412/jack-ma-14-amazing-facts-alibaba-cofounder.htm

105. Sampath Putrevu, "38 quotes by Jack Ma on work, technology, women, and philanthropy," YourStory.com, November 17, 2019, https://yourstory.com/2019/11/jack-ma-quotes-alibaba-singles-day

106. "Jack Ma on the IQ of love - and other top quotes from his Davos interview," World Economic Forum, January 24, 2018, https://www.weforum.org/agenda/2018/01/jack-ma-davos-top-quotes/

107. "Jack Ma on the IQ of love - and other top quotes from his Davos interview," World Economic Forum, January 24, 2018, https://www.weforum.org/agenda/2018/01/jack-ma-davos-top-quotes/

108. Sonia Kolesnikov-Jessop, "Spotlight: Jack Ma, co-founder of Alibaba.com - Business - International Herald Tribune," The New York Times, January 5, 2007, https://www.nytimes.com/2007/01/05/business/worldbusiness/05iht-wbspot06.4109874.html

109. "Alibaba's Jack Ma sees dawn of data-sharing era in global internet age," South China Morning Post, December 3, 2016, https://www.scmp.com/news/china/article/2051287/alibabas-jack-ma-sees-dawn-data-sharing-era-global-internet-age

110. Duncan Clark, "How self-made billionaire Jack Ma used charisma and masterful speaking skills to build the Alibaba empire," April 14, 2016, https://www.businessinsider.com/the-billionaire-founder-of-alibaba-has-been-giving-a-similar-speech-for-17-years-heres-how-he-always-engages-his-audience-2016-4

111. Justin Doebele, "Jack Ma Outlines Bold Vision For His Philanthropy Foundation," Forbes, December 2, 2019, https://www.forbes.com/sites/jdoebele/2019/12/02/jack-ma-shares-his-plans-for-education-philanthropy-in-china/#2b1a8e915c7f

112. Caroline Frost, "Jack Ma, the richest man in China, stepped down as Alibaba chairman — here are 27 of his most brilliant quotes," Business Insider, June 20, 2019, https://markets.businessinsider.com/news/stocks/jack-ma-quotes-alibaba-inspirational-2019-6-1028295089#-a-leader-should-incentivize-but-not-with-money-you-give-trust-respect-appreciation-and-correct-heartfelt-advice-3

113. Sampath Putrevu, "38 quotes by Jack Ma on work, technology, women, and philanthropy," YourStory.com, November 17, 2019, https://yourstory.com/2019/11/jack-ma-quotes-alibaba-singles-day

114. Justin Doebele, "Jack Ma Outlines Bold Vision For His Philanthropy Foundation," Forbes, December 2, 2019, https://www.forbes.com/sites/jdoebele/2019/12/02/jack-ma-shares-his-plans-for-education-philanthropy-in-china/#2b1a8e915c7f

115. Justin Doebele, "Jack Ma Outlines Bold Vision For His Philanthropy Foundation," Forbes, December 2, 2019, https://www.forbes.com/sites/jdoebele/2019/12/02/jack-ma-shares-his-plans-for-education-philanthropy-in-china/#2b1a8e915c7f

116. Rahul R, "Jack Ma Steps Down From Alibaba: His Quotes On AI, Life Are Unmissable," Republic World, September 10, 2019, https://www.republicworld.com/technology-news/apps/jack-ma-steps-down-from-alibaba-his-quotes-on-ai-life-are-unmissable.html

117. "Jack Ma on the IQ of love - and other top quotes from his Davos interview," World Economic Forum, January 24, 2018, https://www.weforum.org/agenda/2018/01/jack-ma-davos-top-quotes/

118. "Jack Ma on the IQ of love - and other top quotes from his Davos interview," World Economic Forum, January 24, 2018, https://www.weforum.org/agenda/2018/01/jack-ma-davos-top-quotes/

119. "Quotable quotes from the World Artificial Intelligence Conference," China Daily, July 10, 2020, https://www.chinadaily.com.cn/a/202007/10/WS5f079cc3a3108348172586df_4.html

120. Sherisse Pham, "Jack Ma: In 30 years, the best CEO could be a robot," CNN Business, April 24, 2017, https://money.cnn.com/2017/04/24/technology/alibaba-jack-ma-30-years-pain-robot-ceo/

121. Caroline Frost, "Jack Ma, the richest man in China, stepped down as Alibaba chairman — here are 27 of his most brilliant quotes," Business Insider, June 20, 2019, https://markets.businessinsider.com/news/stocks/jack-ma-quotes-alibaba-inspirational-2019-6-1028295089#-a-leader-should-incentivize-but-not-with-money-you-give-trust-respect-appreciation-and-correct-heartfelt-advice-3

122. Duncan Clark, Alibaba: The House That Jack Ma Built, 2016

123. William Mellor, Lulu Yilun Chen, Zijing Wu, "Ma Says Alibaba Shareholders Should Feel Love, Not No. 3," Bloomberg, November 9, 2014, https://www.bloomberg.com/news/articles/2014-11-09/ma-says-alibaba-shareholders-should-feel-love-not-no-3

124. Jillian D'Onfro, "15 quotes that show the strange, relentless genius of billionaire Alibaba founder Jack Ma," July 1, 2016, https://www.businessinsider.com/alibaba-founder-jack-ma-quotes-2016-6

125. Laurel J. Delaney, Exporting: The Definitive Guide to Selling Abroad Profitably, 2013

126. Dimitra DeFotis, "5 Lessons From Alibaba's Jack Ma In NYC: Make Technology Great Again!" Barron's, September 20, 2017, https://www.barrons.com/articles/5-lessons-from-alibabas-jack-ma-in-nyc-make-technology-great-again-1505942533

127. Jamil Anderlini, "Person of the year: Jack Ma," The Financial Times, December 12, 2013, https://www.ft.com/content/308e46a8-6189-11e3-916e-00144feabdc0#axzz3139OjXpI

128. Duncan Clark, Alibaba: The House That Jack Ma Built, 2016

129. Sherisse Pham, "Jack Ma: In 30 years, the best CEO could be a robot," CNN Business, April 24, 2017, https://money.cnn.com/2017/04/24/technology/alibaba-jack-ma-30-years-pain-robot-ceo/

130. Tom Brennan, "At Viva Tech, Jack Ma urges using tech for good," Alizila.com, May 16, 2019, https://www.alizila.com/at-viva-tech-jack-ma-urges-using-tech-for-good/

131. William Mellor, Lulu Yilun Chen, Zijing Wu, "Ma Says Alibaba Shareholders Should Feel Love, Not No. 3," Bloomberg, November 9, 2014, https://www.bloomberg.com/news/articles/2014-11-09/ma-says-alibaba-shareholders-should-feel-love-not-no-3

132. Denys Krasnikov, Kostyantyn Chernichkin, "Tech magnate, Alibaba founder Jack Ma praises Ukraine," The Kyiv Post, November 8, 2019, https://www.kyivpost.com/technology/tech-magnate-alibaba-founder-jack-ma-praises-ukraine.html?cn-reloaded=1

133. Caroline Frost, "Jack Ma, the richest man in China, stepped down as Alibaba chairman — here are 27 of his most brilliant quotes," Business Insider, June 20, 2019, https://markets.businessinsider.com/news/stocks/jack-ma-quotes-alibaba-inspirational-2019-6-1028295089#-a-leader-should-incentivize-but-not-with-money-you-give-trust-respect-appreciation-and-correct-heartfelt-advice-3

134. "Jack Ma on the IQ of love - and other top quotes from his Davos interview," World Economic Forum, January 24, 2018, https://www.weforum.org/agenda/2018/01/jack-ma-davos-top-quotes/

135. Duncan Clark, Alibaba: The House That Jack Ma Built, 2016

136. Catherine Clifford, "Alibaba billionaire Jack Ma: Almost 'everybody can be successful if you really try hard,'" CNBC.com, June 4, 2019, https://www.cnbc.com/2019/06/04/alibabas-jack-ma-almost-everyone-can-be-successful.html

137. Lulu Yilun Chen, Tom Mackenzie, "Billionaire Jack Ma Prepares for Life After Alibaba," September 7, 2018, https://www.bloomberg.com/news/articles/2018-09-06/billionaire-jack-ma-prepares-for-life-after-alibaba

138. Sherisse Pham, "Jack Ma: In 30 years, the best CEO could be a robot," CNN Business, April 24, 2017,

    https://money.cnn.com/2017/04/24/technology/alibaba-jack-ma-30-years-pain-robot-ceo/

139. William Mellor, Lulu Yilun Chen, Zijing Wu, "Ma Says Alibaba Shareholders Should Feel Love, Not No. 3," Bloomberg, November 9, 2014, https://www.bloomberg.com/news/articles/2014-11-09/ma-says-alibaba-shareholders-should-feel-love-not-no-3

140. William Mellor, Lulu Yilun Chen, Zijing Wu, "Ma Says Alibaba Shareholders Should Feel Love, Not No. 3," Bloomberg, November 9, 2014, https://www.bloomberg.com/news/articles/2014-11-09/ma-says-alibaba-shareholders-should-feel-love-not-no-3

141. Sampath Putrevu, "38 quotes by Jack Ma on work, technology, women, and philanthropy," YourStory.com, November 17, 2019, https://yourstory.com/2019/11/jack-ma-quotes-alibaba-singles-day

142. Sampath Putrevu, "38 quotes by Jack Ma on work, technology, women, and philanthropy," YourStory.com, November 17, 2019, https://yourstory.com/2019/11/jack-ma-quotes-alibaba-singles-day

143. "Jack Ma and Charlie Rose Gateway '17 Fireside Chat", Alibaba Group, June 20, 2017, https://www.youtube.com/watch?v=ohfA8Hcwvic

144. Sampath Putrevu, "38 quotes by Jack Ma on work, technology, women, and philanthropy," YourStory.com, November 17, 2019, https://yourstory.com/2019/11/jack-ma-quotes-alibaba-singles-day

145. Catherine Clifford, "Alibaba billionaire Jack Ma: Almost 'everybody can be successful if you really try hard,'" CNBC.com, June 4, 2019, https://www.cnbc.com/2019/06/04/alibabas-jack-ma-almost-everyone-can-be-successful.html

146. Yen Nee Lee, "Want to work for Jack Ma? These are the traits he looks for in a candidate," CNBC.com, October 18, 2018, https://www.cnbc.com/2018/10/19/jack-ma-on-hiring-traits-he-looks-for-in-alibaba-job-candidates.html

147. "Future of work: 5 top insights from Davos experts World Economic Forum," World Economic Forum, 25 January,

2019, https://www.weforum.org/agenda/2019/01/future-of-work-tk-top-trends-from-davos/

148. Rahul R, "Jack Ma Steps Down From Alibaba: His Quotes On AI, Life Are Unmissable," Republic World, September 10, 2019, https://www.republicworld.com/technology-news/apps/jack-ma-steps-down-from-alibaba-his-quotes-on-ai-life-are-unmissable.html

149. "10 memorable quotes by Alibaba's Jack Ma," The Economic Times, September 25, 2014, https://economictimes.indiatimes.com/magazines/panache/10-memorable-quotes-by-alibabas-jack-ma/articleshow/43399445.cms

150. Caroline Frost, "Jack Ma, the richest man in China, stepped down as Alibaba chairman — here are 27 of his most brilliant quotes," Business Insider, June 20, 2019, https://markets.businessinsider.com/news/stocks/jack-ma-quotes-alibaba-inspirational-2019-6-1028295089#-a-leader-should-incentivize-but-not-with-money-you-give-trust-respect-appreciation-and-correct-heartfelt-advice-3

151. Sampath Putrevu, "38 quotes by Jack Ma on work, technology, women, and philanthropy," YourStory.com, November 17, 2019, https://yourstory.com/2019/11/jack-ma-quotes-alibaba-singles-day

152. Duncan Clark, Alibaba: The House That Jack Ma Built, 2016

153. Jillian D'Onfro, "15 quotes that show the strange, relentless genius of billionaire Alibaba founder Jack Ma," July 1, 2016, https://www.businessinsider.com/alibaba-founder-jack-ma-quotes-2016-6

154. Caroline Frost, "Jack Ma, the richest man in China, stepped down as Alibaba chairman — here are 27 of his most brilliant quotes," Business Insider, June 20, 2019, https://markets.businessinsider.com/news/stocks/jack-ma-quotes-alibaba-inspirational-2019-6-1028295089#-a-leader-should-incentivize-but-not-with-money-you-give-trust-respect-appreciation-and-correct-heartfelt-advice-3

155. Jillian D'Onfro, "15 quotes that show the strange, relentless genius of billionaire Alibaba founder Jack Ma," July 1, 2016, https://www.businessinsider.com/alibaba-founder-jack-ma-quotes-2016-6

156. "Jack Ma: Love is Important In Business | Davos 2018," World Economic Forum, January 24, 2018, https://www.youtube.com/watch?v=4zzVjonyHcQ

157. Jillian D'Onfro, "15 quotes that show the strange, relentless genius of billionaire Alibaba founder Jack Ma," July 1, 2016, https://www.businessinsider.com/alibaba-founder-jack-ma-quotes-2016-6

158. "10 memorable quotes by Alibaba's Jack Ma," The Economic Times, September 25, 2014, https://economictimes.indiatimes.com/magazines/panache/10-memorable-quotes-by-alibabas-jack-ma/articleshow/43399445.cms

159. Caroline Frost, "Jack Ma, the richest man in China, stepped down as Alibaba chairman — here are 27 of his most brilliant quotes," Business Insider, June 20, 2019, https://markets.businessinsider.com/news/stocks/jack-ma-quotes-alibaba-inspirational-2019-6-1028295089#-a-leader-should-incentivize-but-not-with-money-you-give-trust-respect-appreciation-and-correct-heartfelt-advice-3

160. Rahul R, "Jack Ma Steps Down From Alibaba: His Quotes On AI, Life Are Unmissable," Republic World, September 10, 2019, https://www.republicworld.com/technology-news/apps/jack-ma-steps-down-from-alibaba-his-quotes-on-ai-life-are-unmissable.html

161. Justin Bariso, "Alibaba Founder Jack Ma Says You Don't Need to Know Much to Be Successful. But You Do Need This," Inc., February 15, 2018, https://www.inc.com/justin-bariso/alibaba-founder-jack-ma-just-shared-his-2-step-formula-for-success-and-its-absolutely-brilliant.html

162. Caroline Frost, "Jack Ma, the richest man in China, stepped down as Alibaba chairman — here are 27 of his most brilliant quotes," Business Insider, June 20, 2019, https://markets.businessinsider.com/news/stocks/jack-ma-quotes-alibaba-inspirational-2019-6-1028295089#-a-leader-should-incentivize-but-not-with-money-you-give-trust-respect-appreciation-and-correct-heartfelt-advice-3

163. "Jack Ma: Love is Important In Business | Davos 2018," World Economic Forum, January 24, 2018, https://www.youtube.com/watch?v=4zzVjonyHcQ

164. Zameena Mejia, "Self-made billionaire Jack Ma: How to be successful in your 20s, 30s, 40s and beyond," CNBC, January 30, 2018, https://www.cnbc.com/2018/01/30/jack-ma-dont-fear-making-mistakes-in-your-20s-and-30s.html

165. Caroline Frost, "Jack Ma, the richest man in China, stepped down as Alibaba chairman — here are 27 of his most brilliant quotes," Business Insider, June 20, 2019, https://markets.businessinsider.com/news/stocks/jack-ma-quotes-alibaba-inspirational-2019-6-1028295089#-a-leader-should-incentivize-but-not-with-money-you-give-trust-respect-appreciation-and-correct-heartfelt-advice-3

166. Bhavya Kaushal, "Know the Tricks of the Trade from the Undisputed King of Business: Jack Ma," Entrepreneur, October 31, 2018, https://www.entrepreneur.com/slideshow/322603

167. "Jack Ma's advice to millennials: Find a good boss in your 20s, 30s. Here's why," POLITICO, October 25, 2017, https://politics.com.ph/jack-mas-advice-millennials-find-good-boss-20s-30s-heres/

168. Rahul R, "Jack Ma Steps Down From Alibaba: His Quotes On AI, Life Are Unmissable,"

169. Republic World, September 10, 2019, https://www.republicworld.com/technology-news/apps/jack-ma-steps-down-from-alibaba-his-quotes-on-ai-life-are-unmissable.html

170. Sampath Putrevu, "38 quotes by Jack Ma on work, technology, women, and philanthropy," YourStory.com, November 17, 2019, https://yourstory.com/2019/11/jack-ma-quotes-alibaba-singles-day

171. Jolene Hee, "'We Were Actually Very Silly': Billionaire Jack Ma On Success, Luck & Speaking Harsh Truths," Vulcan Post, May 22, 2015, https://vulcanpost.com/246691/jack-ma-success-luck-speaking-harsh-truths/

172. Caroline Frost, "Jack Ma, the richest man in China, stepped down as Alibaba chairman — here are 27 of his most brilliant quotes," Business Insider, June 20, 2019, https://markets.businessinsider.com/news/stocks/jack-ma-quotes-alibaba-inspirational-2019-6-1028295089#-a-

leader-should-incentivize-but-not-with-money-you-give-trust-respect-appreciation-and-correct-heartfelt-advice-3

173. "Interview Jack Ma – Alibaba.com," Talk Asia, CNN, April 25, 2006, https://edition.cnn.com/2006/WORLD/asiapcf/04/24/talk asia.ma.script/

174. Tom Brennan, "At Viva Tech, Jack Ma urges using tech for good," Alizila.com, May 16, 2019, https://www.alizila.com/at-viva-tech-jack-ma-urges-using-tech-for-good/

175. Everett Rosenfeld, "Jack Ma to US: Quit worrying so much about China," CNBC, September 30, 2015, https://www.cnbc.com/2015/09/30/us-quit-worrying-so-much-about-china.html

176. "Do sleep, don't have doubts. Jack Ma's guide to sanity and success," World Economic Forum, January 23, 2019, https://wef.ch/2R9983S

177. "Do sleep, don't have doubts. Jack Ma's guide to sanity and success," World Economic Forum, January 23, 2019, https://wef.ch/2R9983S

178. Wilson Lee Flores, "Life & success secrets of the humble billionaire Jack Ma," The Philippine Star, October 28, 2017, https://www.philstar.com/lifestyle/sunday-life/2017/10/28/1753386/life-success-secrets-humble-billionaire-jack-ma

179. "Jack Ma on the IQ of love - and other top quotes from his Davos interview," World Economic Forum, January 24, 2018, https://www.weforum.org/agenda/2018/01/jack-ma-davos-top-quotes/

180. Sampath Putrevu, "38 quotes by Jack Ma on work, technology, women, and philanthropy," YourStory.com, November 17, 2019, https://yourstory.com/2019/11/jack-ma-quotes-alibaba-singles-day

181. Li Yuan, "Jack Ma Is Retiring From Alibaba. He Won't Go Far.," The New York Times, September 10, 2019, https://www.nytimes.com/2019/09/10/business/alibaba-jack-ma-retire.html

182. Jolene Hee, "'We Were Actually Very Silly': Billionaire Jack Ma On Success, Luck & Speaking Harsh Truths," Vulcan Post, May 22, 2015, https://vulcanpost.com/246691/jack-ma-success-luck-speaking-harsh-truths/

183. Jackie Wattles, "How Jack Ma went from English teacher to tech billionaire," CNN Business, September 9, 2018, https://money.cnn.com/2018/09/09/technology/business/jack-ma-alibaba-bio/index.html

184. "10 memorable quotes by Alibaba's Jack Ma," The Economic Times, September 25, 2014, https://economictimes.indiatimes.com/magazines/panache/10-memorable-quotes-by-alibabas-jack-ma/articleshow/43399445.cms

185. Sampath Putrevu, "38 quotes by Jack Ma on work, technology, women, and philanthropy," YourStory.com, November 17, 2019, https://yourstory.com/2019/11/jack-ma-quotes-alibaba-singles-day

186. John Smith, "10 Best Motivational Quotes on Success by Jack MA," Medium, September 12, 2019, https://medium.com/@videomonk75/10-best-motivational-quotes-on-success-by-jack-ma-814c6df15e35

187. Catherine Clifford, "Alibaba billionaire Jack Ma: Almost 'everybody can be successful if you really try hard,'" CNBC.com, June 4, 2019, https://www.cnbc.com/2019/06/04/alibabas-jack-ma-almost-everyone-can-be-successful.html

188. Bhavya Kaushal, "Know the Tricks of the Trade from the Undisputed King of Business: Jack Ma," Entrepreneur, October 31, 2018, https://www.entrepreneur.com/slideshow/322603

189. Jillian D'Onfro, "15 quotes that show the strange, relentless genius of billionaire Alibaba founder Jack Ma," July 1, 2016, https://www.businessinsider.com/alibaba-founder-jack-ma-quotes-2016-6

190. Sampath Putrevu, "38 quotes by Jack Ma on work, technology, women, and philanthropy," YourStory.com, November 17, 2019, https://yourstory.com/2019/11/jack-ma-quotes-alibaba-singles-day

191. Josh Horwitz, "Alibaba has come to Detroit to sell small businesses the Chinese dream," Quartz, June 19, 2017, https://qz.com/1006682/at-alibaba-gateway-17-in-detroit-chinas-e-commerce-giant-is-building-its-brand-with-us-small-businesses/

192. "Jack Ma on the IQ of love - and other top quotes from his Davos interview," World Economic Forum, January 24, 2018, https://www.weforum.org/agenda/2018/01/jack-ma-davos-top-quotes/

193. Justin Doebele, "Jack Ma Outlines Bold Vision For His Philanthropy Foundation," Forbes, December 2, 2019, https://www.forbes.com/sites/jdoebele/2019/12/02/jack-ma-shares-his-plans-for-education-philanthropy-in-china/#2b1a8e915c7f

194. Sampath Putrevu, "38 quotes by Jack Ma on work, technology, women, and philanthropy," YourStory.com, November 17, 2019, https://yourstory.com/2019/11/jack-ma-quotes-alibaba-singles-day

195. Tom Brennan, "At Viva Tech, Jack Ma urges using tech for good," Alizila.com, May 16, 2019, https://www.alizila.com/at-viva-tech-jack-ma-urges-using-tech-for-good/

196. Sonia Kolesnikov-Jessop, "Spotlight: Jack Ma, co-founder of Alibaba.com - Business - International Herald Tribune," The New York Times, January 5, 2007, https://www.nytimes.com/2007/01/05/business/worldbusiness/05iht-wbspot06.4109874.html

197. "Watch Jack Ma at Viva Tech 2019," Alibaba Group, May 16, 2019, https://www.youtube.com/watch?v=g1Y05cuekIs

198. Duncan Clark, "How self-made billionaire Jack Ma used charisma and masterful speaking skills to build the Alibaba empire," April 14, 2016, https://www.businessinsider.com/the-billionaire-founder-of-alibaba-has-been-giving-a-similar-speech-for-17-years-heres-how-he-always-engages-his-audience-2016-4

199. "Do sleep, don't have doubts. Jack Ma's guide to sanity and success," World Economic Forum, January 23, 2019, https://wef.ch/2R9983S

## Follow me on social media:

https://twitter.com/olivia_longray
https://facebook.com/olivia.longray
https://instagram.com/olivia_longray
https://t.me/olivia_longray

Cover photo by Konstantin Melnitskiy

www.ingramcontent.com/pod-product-compliance
Lightning Source LLC
Chambersburg PA
CBHW070435220526
45466CB00004B/1691